doll Tees
Stamps & Stencils

Create designs that
are sure to shine!

by **Emily Osborn**

D0731620

AmericanGirl

Published by American Girl Publishing
Copyright © 2016 American Girl

Questions or comments? Call 1-800-845-0005,
visit **americangirl.com,** or write to Customer Service,
American Girl, 8400 Fairway Place, Middleton, WI 53562-0497.

Printed in China
16 17 18 19 20 21 22 LEO 10 9 8 7 6 5 4 3 2 1

All American Girl marks and Truly Me™ are trademarks of American Girl.

Editorial Development: Emily Osborn
Art Direction and Design: Gretchen Becker, Lisa Wilber
Production: Jeannette Bailey, Laura Markowitz, Cynthia Stiles, Kristi Tabrizi
Photography: Joe Hinrichs, Jeff Rockwell, Youa Thao
Craft Styling: Emily Osborn
Set Styling: Casey Hull, Kim Sphar, Emma Wimberley
Doll Styling: Karen Timm, Meghan Hurley
Illustrations: Flávia Conley and Monika Roe

Dear Doll Lover,

No matter what your style, T-shirts and tanks are in during every season, and can be designed in different ways to be trendy or even ahead of the fashion curve. This book will help you create multiple "top" fashions for your doll.

Practice your designs on the T-shirt notepad before finalizing a shirt. Use the kit's stencils to create dozens of fun and funky designs perfect for outings, from parties to picnics.

Or create stamps using everyday items like toilet paper rolls, pencil erasers, or vegetables to style animals, flowers, or patterns. Find your favorite style, pattern, or idea and make your doll her very own fashion statement!

Time to shine!

Your friends at American Girl

Craft with Care

Keep Your Doll and Pet Safe

When creating doll or pet crafts, remember that dyes from ribbons, felt, beads, cords, fabrics, fleece, paint, and other supplies may bleed onto your doll and pet or their clothes and leave permanent stains. To help prevent this, use lighter colors when possible, and check your doll and her pet often to make sure the colors aren't transferring to their bodies, vinyl, or clothes or to the pet's fur. And never get your doll or pet wet! Water and heat greatly increase dye rub-off. Use **fabric paint** for all of your T-shirt paint designs, and let dry for at least 24 hours before putting the shirt on your doll. For extra protection, place a piece of white sticky felt on the inside of the shirt before your doll wears it, to help prevent staining.

Get Help!

When you see this symbol ✋ in the book, it means that you need an adult to help you with all or a part of the craft. ALWAYS ask for help before continuing.

Ask First

If a craft asks you to use any old item, such as a shirt or sock, always ask an adult for permission before you use it. Your parent might still need it, so check first.

Craft Smart

If a craft instruction says "cut," use scissors. If it says "glue," use craft glue or adhesive dots. And if it says "paint," use a nontoxic acrylic paint. Before you use these supplies, ask an adult to check them over—especially paints and glues. Some crafting supplies are not safe for kids.

Put Up Crafts and Supplies

When you're not using the crafts or art supplies, put them up high or store them away from little kids and pets. Toddlers and animals might eat your crafts, break them, or even hurt themselves when playing with them.

WARNING

Safely tuck your doll away while you create art for her so that paint, glue, and other messy craft supplies don't get on your doll or her clothes. Make sure each art project dries completely before using it near your doll.

T-SHIRT TIP
Don't stretch the purple tank! Pull it up over your doll's feet to dress her.

Tape Tees

Every tee will be fun and unique with this simple taping technique.

Rainbow Stripes

Place tape on a shirt in random lines. Paint the sections of the shirt that are still visible. Once the paint is dry, pull up the tape to reveal a unique and colorful design.

Horizontal Stripes

Place tape in equally spaced horizontal lines across the shirt. Paint the stripes of the tee that are still visible. Allow the paint to dry. Then pull up the tape to see your fun striped tee.

TP Tees

Turn ordinary toilet paper rolls into fun shapes to make these designs.

Flower

Gently flatten a toilet paper roll so the ends are slightly pointy on two sides, creating the shape of a petal. Dip one end of the roll in paint. Stamp the roll onto the shirt. Repeat this, slightly moving the position of the roll each time to form a flower. Try to keep one point of the roll in the same spot each time to make the center of the flower. Use the same color, or try a different color for each petal.

Bunny

Dip one end of a toilet paper roll into paint, and stamp a circle onto the bottom center of a shirt. This is the bunny's face. Flatten a second roll (as for the flower, above). Dip one end of that roll into paint, and stamp two petals above the circle. These are the bunny's ears. Paint the inside of the ears. Then paint on a nose and mouth. Let dry. Glue googly eyes onto its face.

Pumpkin Tee

1. Dip one end of a **toilet paper roll** into **orange paint** and stamp it onto your shirt.

2. Then stamp two more circles, overlapping with the first one.

3. Paint the outer parts of the circles **dark orange** and the entire middle circle **light orange** to show the sections of the pumpkin. Using **brown paint,** make a stem. Let dry.

4. Place the **pumpkin leaf stencil** on the pumpkin near the stem. Using **green paint,** paint the leaf onto the pumpkin. Let dry.

Rock 'n' Roller Tees

Your doll will be a star in these lint-roller fashions.

Hearts or Stars

Stick heart or star (or any shape) craft foam pieces onto a mini lint roller in a pattern of your choosing. With a paint brush, paint only the craft foam pieces on the roller. Try not to get paint on the roller itself to avoid smudging on the shirt. While the paint is still wet, roll the lint roller across the shirt. Go slowly and press firmly for the best results. Let dry.

Big on Bugs

These bee-you-tee-ful shirts are sure to spin a web of compliments.

Bee You Tee

For this tee, use a small papier-mâché hexagon-shaped box. Dip or paint the edges of the box; then stamp it onto the shirt. Reapply the paint, and stamp again, aligning one edge of the box with one edge of the hexagon-shape already on the tee. Repeat until the entire shirt is covered and looks like a honeycomb. Let dry. If you'd like, paint three of the hexagons for an extra pop of color. Once dry, add a cute bee sticker.

Spiderweb

Place the spiderweb stencil onto a shirt. With a paintbrush, paint the stencil. Let dry. Then lift the stencil up to reveal the spiderweb. Place a silly spider sticker onto the web to complete the look.

Starburst Stamp Tee

1. Cut a star shape out of **duct tape**.

2. Place the star in the center of the tee.

3. Dip **pencil eraser** in **paint**. Then stamp it on the edge and around the stencil. Use multiple colors if you'd like.

4. When you feel you have enough paint on the shirt, lift the stencil to reveal the star shape.

Pencil Pushers

Pick up your pencils and prepare for some creative designs.

Flower Pattern

Rubberband seven unsharpened pencils together in a flower shape. Dip the eraser ends into paint, and stamp them onto the shirt. Wipe the eraser ends off with a damp paper towel until there's no more paint on them. Then dip the eraser ends in a different paint color and stamp on the shirt. Repeat for a third flower. To create the stems, take a blunt-ended toothpick and dip it lengthwise in green paint. Press the paint-covered toothpick vertically underneath each flower. Finally, place leaf-shaped adhesive gems on each stem for extra decoration.

Heart Stencil

Place the heart stencil onto the shirt. Dip the eraser end of an unsharpened pencil into light pink paint. Stamp the eraser inside and on the edges of the heart stencil, focusing the light color toward the top of the heart. Dip the eraser in more paint as needed. Change the paint color to a medium pink, focusing the stamp toward the middle of the heart. Then use a dark pink or red paint for the bottom section of the heart. Once dry, lift the stencil off the shirt to reveal the multicolored heart.

Personalize It!

Use the alphabet stencil to paint a letter or two on your tee to make it your own.

BFF

Place the "B" stencil onto the shirt. Paint the stencil and let dry. Lift the stencil. Repeat twice with the "F" stencil, allowing time to dry each time to avoid smudging. Then take the arrow stencil and place it under the "BFF" letters. Paint inside the arrow stencil and let dry before lifting the stencil off the shirt. Make a second shirt for your doll's best friend. Make sure to paint the arrow facing the opposite direction so they point toward each other.

Monogram

Paint the first letter of your doll's name on a shirt. It can be in the upper right-hand or left-hand corner of the tee, or even the center. Whichever letter you choose, to get crisp lines, let the paint dry before lifting the stencil.

Texting Tees

These shirts have a lot to say.

LOL, LUV, and YAY

Use the alphabet stencils to create three-letter text messages of your choice. We chose LOL (laugh out loud), LUV (love), and YAY (yay!). Remember to paint one letter at a time, allowing time to dry before lifting the stencil to avoid smudging the paint.

Feathered Friends

Set your sights sky-high with this collection.

It's Owl Good

This shirt is a hoot! Use the owl stencil to create this design. Place the stencil in the center of the tee and paint with a color of your choice. Let dry. Lift the stencil and glue googly eyes on top of the stenciled ones for extra personality, if you wish.

Sweet Tweet

This tee is simple yet sweet. Place the bird stencil in the center of your shirt and paint the shape with baby blue or a color of your choosing. Once dry, lift the stencil off the shirt. Glue a tiny googly eye on the bird as a finishing touch.

Watermelon Tee

1.  Ask an adult to cut a **potato** into quarters.

2. Take one potato quarter and dip it into **pink paint.** Stamp the potato onto a shirt. Let dry.

3. Use a **paintbrush** and **green paint** to paint a green border on the curved part of the watermelon.

4. Dip the blunt end of the paintbrush in **brown or black paint** and paint dots onto the watermelon. Let dry.

Play with Your Food

Make shirts that are perfect for a picnic in the park.

Lucky Girl

Ask an adult to cut the end off a green pepper. Dip the cut side of the pepper in green paint and stamp it onto a shirt. Use a thin paintbrush to paint a stem onto the clover. Let dry.

An Apple a Day

Ask an adult to cut a small apple in half. Dip one half of the apple, including the stem, into red or green paint. (If it is easier, you may choose to brush the paint onto the apple instead of dipping it.) Press the painted apple firmly onto the shirt. Lift it up slowly. Let dry. Place the apple leaf stencil on the apple, near its stem. Using green or brown paint, paint the leaf onto the shirt. Let dry. Then peel the stencil up to see your fruity design.

The Sky's the Limit

Shine on and stand out in these celestial designs.

Rainbow

Place the rainbow stencil on a shirt. Paint each line of the rainbow a different color. Paint the clouds white, silver, or another color of your choosing. Let dry. Slowly lift the stencil.

Night Sky

Place the moon and stars stencil in the center of a shirt. Paint your stencil with yellow, gold, or silver paint and let dry. Peel the stencil slowly off the shirt.

Sunny Day

Place the sun stencil in the center of a shirt. Mix orange, yellow, and gold sparkle paint for a sunny color concoction. Paint the sun shape. Let dry and slowly lift the stencil. For extra designing fun, combine the sun stencil with the Pencil Pusher flower design, or paint a smiley face on it.

Spring Umbrella Tee

1. Place the **umbrella stencil** in the center of a shirt.

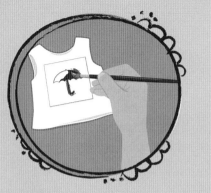

2. **Paint** the umbrella onto the shirt. Let dry.

3. Peel the stencil off the shirt.

4. Attach **raindrop-shaped adhesive gems** around the umbrella for a fashion-forward design.

Fair Weather Fashions

These shirts are set for any weather—rain or shine!

Winter Mittens

In sleet or snow, this shirt will keep a warm smile on your doll's face. Place the mittens stencil in the center of a shirt. Paint the mittens shapes and let dry. Lift the stencil. Glue fun gems onto your mittens for added flair.

Summer Flip-Flops

It's easy to dress for summer with this flip-flops fashion. Place the flip-flops stencil on the shirt. Paint the flip-flops shapes onto the tee and let dry. Lift the stencil. Your doll is now ready to go to the beach in style.

Cheer Gear

Show off your school spirit at pep rallies or the big game.

#1

Let your doll's inner sports fan come out with this number one tee. Using the "#1" stencil, paint and let dry. Lift the stencil.

Megaphone

Place the megaphone stencil on a shirt. Paint the stencil with a bright color. Let dry. Lift the stencil from the shirt to let your doll's inner cheerleader shine.

Go Team!

With this shirt, your doll can show her team spirit. Position the "Go Team!" stencil on a shirt. Paint the stencil in your doll's team colors. After the paint is dry, remove the stencil.

Winged Wonders

Let your creativity soar with these inspiring insects.

Butterfly

Your doll will want to spread her wings in this transforming tee. Place the butterfly stencil on the tee. Use multiple colors to paint a brilliant butterfly. Once dry, lift the stencil.

Dragonfly

Position the dragonfly stencil on a shirt. Paint the wings a sparkly color and the dragonfly's body a solid color. Let dry. Lift the stencil.

Show us your styles!

Share a picture of your doll's favorite tee!

Doll Tees: Stamps and Stencils **Editor**
American Girl
8400 Fairway Place
Middleton, WI 53562

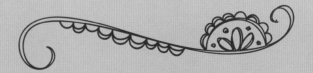

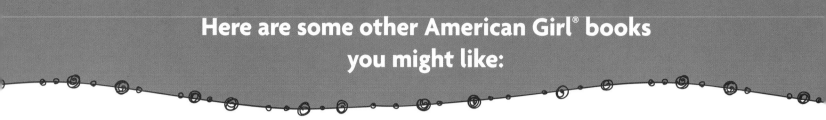

Here are some other American Girl® books
you might like:

Each sold separately. Find more books online at americangirl.com.